Three Articles o1

Society for Pure English

(Contributor: A. Clutton-Brock,

Elizabeth Bridges Daryush, H. W. Fowler)

Alpha Editions

This edition published in 2023

ISBN : 9789357945547

Design and Setting By
Alpha Editions
www.alphaedis.com
Email - info@alphaedis.com

Contents

I. NOTES ON THE FUNCTION OF METAPHOR

The business of the writer is to arouse in the mind of his reader the fullest possible consciousness of the ideas or emotion that he is expressing.

To this end he suggests a comparison between it and something else which is similar to it in respect of those qualities to which he desires to draw attention. The reader's mind at once gets to work unconsciously on this comparison, rejecting the unlike qualities and recognizing with an enhanced and satisfied consciousness the like ones. The functions of simile and metaphor are the same in this respect.

Both simile and metaphor are best when not too close to the idea they express, that is, when they have not many qualities in common with it which are not cogent to the aspect under consideration.

The test of a well-used metaphor is that it should completely fulfil this function: there should be no by-products of imagery which distract from the poet's aim, and vitiate and weaken the desired consciousness.

A simile, in general, need not be so close as a metaphor, because the point of resemblance is indicated, whereas in a metaphor this is left to the reader to discover.

When a simile or metaphor is from the material to the immaterial, or vice versa, the analogy should be more complete than when it is between two things on the same plane: when they are on different planes there is less dullness (that is, less failure to produce consciousness), and the greater mental effort required of the reader warrants some assistance.

The degree of effort required in applying any given metaphor should be in relation to the degree of emotion proper to the passage in which it is used. Only those metaphors which require little or no mental exertion should be used in very emotional passages, or the emotional effect will be much weakened: a far-fetched, abstruse metaphor or simile implies that the writer is at leisure from his emotion, and suggests this attitude in the reader.—[E.B.]

II. SOME NOTES ON METAPHOR IN JOURNALISM

Live and dead metaphor; some pitfalls; self-consciousness and mixed metaphor.

1. Live and Dead Metaphor.

In all discussion of metaphor it must be borne in mind that some metaphors are living, i.e. are offered and accepted with a consciousness of their nature as substitutes for their literal equivalents, while others are dead, i.e. have been so often used that speaker and hearer have ceased to be aware that the words are not literal: but the line of distinction between the live and the dead is a shifting one, the dead being sometimes liable, under the stimulus of an affinity or a repulsion, to galvanic stirrings indistinguishable from life. Thus, in *The men were sifting meal* we have a literal use of *sift*; in *Satan hath desired to have you, that he may sift you as wheat*, 'sift' is a live metaphor; in *the sifting of evidence*, the metaphor is so familiar that it is about equal chances whether *sifting* or *examination* will be used, and a sieve is not present to the thought— unless, indeed, some one conjures it up by saying *All the evidence must first be sifted with acid tests*, or *with the microscope*; under such a stimulus our metaphor turns out to have been not dead, but dormant. The other word, *examine*, will do well enough as an example of the real stone-dead metaphor; the Latin *examino*, being from *examen* the tongue of a balance, meant originally to weigh; but, though weighing is not done with acid tests or microscopes any more than sifting, *examine* gives no convulsive twitchings, like *sift*, at finding itself in their company; *examine*, then, is dead metaphor, and *sift* only half dead, or three-quarters.

2. Some pitfalls. A, Unsustained Metaphor; B, Overdone Metaphor; C, Spoilt Metaphor; D, Battles of the Dead; E, Mixed Metaphor.

A. Unsustained Metaphor

He was still in the middle of those twenty years of neglect which only began to lift in 1868. The plunge into metaphor at *lift*, which presupposes a mist, is too sudden after the literal *twenty years of neglect*; years, even gloomy years, do not lift.

The means of education at the disposal of the Protestants and Presbyterians of the North were stunted and sterilized. 'The means at disposal' names something too little vegetable or animal to consort with the metaphorical verbs. Education (personified) may be stunted, but means may not.

The measure of Mr. Asquith's shame does not consist in the mere fact that he has announced his intention to ... Metaphorical measuring, like literal, requires a more accommodating instrument than a stubborn fact.

B. Overdone Metaphor

The days are perhaps past when a figure was deliberately chosen that could be worked out with line upon line of relentless detail, and the following well-known specimen is from Richardson:—

Tost to and fro by the high winds of passionate control, I behold the desired port, the single state, into which I would fain steer; but am kept off by the foaming billows of a brother's and sister's envy, and by the raging winds of a supposed invaded authority; while I see in Lovelace, the rocks on one hand, and in Solmes, the sands on the other; and tremble, lest I should split upon the former or strike upon the latter.

The present fashion is rather to develop a metaphor only by way of burlesque. All that need be asked of those who tend to this form of satire is to remember that, while some metaphors do seem to deserve such treatment, the number of times that the same joke can safely be made, even with variations, is limited; the limit has surely been exceeded, for instance, with 'the long arm of coincidence'; what proportion may this triplet of quotations bear to the number of times the thing has been done?—*The long arm of coincidence throws the Slifers into Mercedes's Cornish garden a little too heavily. The author does not strain the muscles of coincidence's arm to bring them into relation. Then the long arm of coincidence rolled up its sleeves and set to work with a rapidity and vigour which defy description.*

Modern overdoing, apart from burlesque, is chiefly accidental, and results not from too much care, but from too little. *The most irreconcilable of Irish landlords are beginning to recognize that we are on the eve of the dawn of a new day in Ireland.* 'On the eve of' is a dead metaphor for 'about to experience', and to complete it with 'the dawn of a day' is as bad as to say, *It cost one pound sterling, ten* instead of *one pound ten.*

C. Spoilt Metaphor

The essential merit of real or live metaphor being to add vividness to what is being conveyed, it need hardly be said that accuracy of detail is even more necessary in metaphorical than in literal expressions; the habit of metaphor, however, and the habit of accuracy do not always go together.

Yet Taurès was the Samson who upheld the pillars of the Bloc.

Yet what more distinguished names does the Anglican Church of the last reign boast than those of F.D. Maurice, Kingsley, Stanley, Robertson of Brighton, and even, if we will draw our net a little wider, the great Arnold?

He was the very essence of cunning, the incarnation of a book-thief.

Samson's way with pillars was not to uphold them; we draw nets closer, but cast them wider; and what is the incarnation of a thief? too, too solid flesh indeed!

D. Battles of Dead Metaphors

In *The Covenanters took up arms* there is no metaphor; in *The Covenanters flew to arms* there is one only—*flew to* for *quickly took up*; in *She flew to arms in defence of her darling* there are two, the arms being now metaphorical as well as the flying; moreover, the two metaphors are separate ones; but, being dead, and also not inconsistent with each other, they lie together quietly enough. But dead metaphors will not lie quietly together if there was repugnance between them in life; e'en in their ashes live their wonted fires, and they get up and fight.

It is impossible to crush the Government's aim to restore the means of living and working freely. 'Crush' for baffle, 'aim' for purpose, are both dead metaphors so long as they are kept apart, but the juxtaposition forces on us the thought that you cannot crush an aim.

National military training is the bedrock on which alone we can hope to carry through the great struggles which the future may have in store for us. 'Bedrock' and 'carry through' are both moribund or dormant, but not stone-dead.

The vogue of the motor-car seems destined to help forward the provision of good road-communication, a feature which is sadly in arrear. Good road-communication may be a feature, and it may be in arrear, and yet a feature cannot be in arrear; things that are equal to the same thing may be equal to each other in geometry, but language is not geometry.

They are cyphers living under the *shadow* of a great man.

He stood, his feet *glued* to the spot, his eyes *riveted* on the heavens.

The Geddes report is to be *emasculated* a little in the Cabinet, and then *thrown* at the heads of the Electorate.

Viscount Grey's suggestion may, in spite of everything, prove the *nucleus* of *solution*.

The superior stamina of the Oxonian told in no *half-hearted measure.* [Even careful writers are sometimes unaware of the comical effect of some chance juxtaposition of words and ideas, whereby a dormant metaphor is set on its legs. Thus Leslie Stephen in his life of Swift wrote: *Sir William Temple, though he seems to have been vigorous and in spite of gout a brisk walker, was approaching his grave.* And again when he was triumphantly recording the progress of agnosticism he has: *Even the high-churchmen have thrown the Flood overboard.* [ED.]]

E. Mixed Metaphors

- 4 -

For the examples given in D, tasteless word-selection is a fitter description than mixed metaphor, since each of the words that conflict with others is not intended, as a metaphor at all. 'Mixed metaphor' is more appropriate when one or both of the terms can only be consciously metaphorical. Little warning is needed against it; it is so conspicuous as seldom to get into speech or print undetected.

This is not the time to throw up the sponge, when the enemy, already weakened and divided, are on the run to a new defensive position. A mixture of prize-ring and battlefield.

In the following extract from a speech it is difficult to be sure how many times metaphors are mixed; readers versed in the mysteries of oscillation may be able to decide:

No society, no community, can place its house in such a condition that it is always on a rock, oscillating between solvency and insolvency. What I have to do is to see that our house is built upon a solid foundation, never allowing the possibility of the Society's life-blood being sapped. Just in proportion as you are careful in looking after the condition of your income, just in proportion as you deal with them carefully, will the solidarity of the Society's financial condition remain intact. Immediately you begin to play fast and loose with your income the first blow at your financial stability will have been struck.

A real poet losing himself in the *meshes* of a foolish *obsession*.

Johnson tore the *hearts* out of books ruthlessly in order to extract the *honey* out of them expeditiously. Are we to let the *pendulum* swing back to the old *rut?* Those little houses at the top of the street, *dwarfed* by the *grandiloquence* on the opposite side, are too small, too.

3. Self-consciousness and Mixed Metaphor.

The gentlemen of the Press regularly devote a small percentage of their time to accusing each other of mixing metaphors or announcing that they are themselves about to do so (What a mixture of metaphors! If we may mix our metaphors. To change the metaphor), the offence apparently being not to mix them, but to be unaware that you have done it. The odd thing is that, whether he is on the offensive or the defensive, the writer who ventures to talk of mixing metaphors often shows that he does not know what mixed metaphor is. Two typical examples of the offensive follow:

_The *Scotsman* says: 'The crowded benches of the Ministerialists contain the germs of disintegration. A more ill-assorted majority could hardly be conceived, and presently the Opposition must realize of what small account is the manoeuvring of the Free-Fooders or of any other section of the party. If the sling be only properly handled, the new Parliamentary Goliath will be overthrown easily enough. The stone for the sling must, however, be found on the Ministerial side of the House, and not on the Opposition side.'

Apparently the stone for the sling will be a germ. But doubtless mixed feelings lead to mixed metaphors._ In this passage, we are well rid of the germs before we hear of the sling, and the mixture of metaphors is quite imaginary.

Since literal benches often contain literal germs, but 'crowded benches' and 'germs of disintegration' are here separate metaphors for a numerous party and tendencies to disunion, our critic had ready to his hand in the first sentence, if he had but known it, something much more like a mixture of metaphors than what he mistakes for one.

'When the Chairman of Committees—a politician of their own hue—allowed Mr. Maddison to move his amendment in favour of secular education, a decision which was not quite in accordance with precedent, the floodgates of sectarian controversy were opened, and the apple of discord—the endowment of the gospel of Cowper-Temple—was thrown into the midst of the House of Commons.' What a mixture of metaphor! One pictures this gospel-apple battling with the stream released by the opened floodgates. In point of fact, the floodgates and the apple are successive metaphors, unmixed; the mixing of them is done by the critic himself, not by the criticized; and as to *gospel-apple*, by which it is hinted that the mixture is triple, the original writer had merely mentioned in the *gospel* phrase the thing compared by the side of what it is compared to, as when one explains *the Athens of the North* by adding *Edinburgh.*

Writers who are on the defensive apologize for *change* and *mixture* of metaphors as though one was as bad as the other; the two sins are in fact entirely different; a man may change his metaphors as often as he likes; it is for him to judge whether the result will or will not be unpleasantly florid; but he should not ask our leave to do it; if the result is bad, his apology will not mend matters, and if it is not bad no apology was called for. On the other hand, to mix metaphors, if the mixture is real, is an offence that should have been not apologized for, but avoided. Whichever the phrase, the motive is the same—mortal fear of being accused of mixed metaphor.

...showed that Free Trade could provide the jam without recourse being had to Protective food-taxes: next came a period in which (to mix our metaphors) the jam was a nice slice of tariff pie for everybody, but then came the Edinburgh Compromise, by which the jam for the towns was that there were to be... When *jam* is used in three successive sentences in its hackneyed sense of consolation, it need hardly be considered in the middle one of them a live metaphor at all; however, the as-good-as-dead metaphor of jam *is* capable of being stimulated into life if any one is so foolish as to bring into contact with it another half-dead metaphor of its own (i.e. of the foodstuff) kind, and it *was*, after all, mixing metaphors to say the jam was a slice of pie; but then the way of escape was to withdraw either the

jam or the pie, instead of forcing them together down our throats with a ramrod of apology.

Time sifts the richest granary, and posterity is a dainty feeder. But Lyall's words, at any rate—to mix the metaphor—will escape the blue pencil even of such drastic editors as they. Since all three metaphors are live ones, and *they* are the sifter and the feeder, the working of these into grammatical connexion with the blue pencil does undoubtedly mix metaphors. But then our author gives us to understand that he knows he is doing it, and surely that is enough. Even so some liars reckon that a lie is no disgrace provided that they wink at a bystander as they tell it, even so those who are addicted to the phrase 'to use a vulgarism' expect to achieve the feat of being at once vulgar and superior to vulgarity.

Certainly we cannot detect the suggested lack of warmth in the speech as it is printed, for in his speech, as in the Prime Minister's, it seems to us that (if we may change the metaphor) exactly the right note was struck.

We may, on the one hand, receive into our gill its precise content of the complex mixture that fills the puncheon of the whole world's literature, on the other—to change the metaphor—our few small strings may thrill in sympathetic harmony to some lyrical zephyrs and remain practically unresponsive to the deep-sea gale of Aeschylus or Dante.

Why, yes, gentlemen, you may change your metaphors, if it seems good to you, but you may also be pretty sure that, if you feel the necessity of proclaiming the change, you had better have abstained from it.

Two of the trump cards played against the Bill are (1) that 'it makes every woman who pays a tax-collector in her own house', and (2) that 'it will destroy happy domestic relations in hundreds of thousands of homes'; if we may at once change our metaphor, these are the notes which are most consistently struck in the stream of letters, now printed day by day for our edification in the Mail. This writer need not have asked our leave to change from cards to music; he is within his rights, anyhow, and the odds are, indeed, that if he had not reminded us of the cards we should have forgotten them in the intervening lines, but how did a person so sensitive to change of metaphor fail to reflect that it is ill playing the piano in the water? 'A stream of letters', it is true, is only a picturesque way of saying 'many letters', and ordinarily a dead metaphor; but once put your seemingly dead yet picturesque metaphor close to a piano that is being played, and its notes wake the dead— at any rate for readers who have just had the word *metaphor* called to their memory.—H.W. FOWLER.

III. DEAD METAPHORS

Metaphor becomes a habit with writers who wish to express more emotion than they feel, and who employ it as an ornament to statements that should be made plainly or not at all. Used thus, it is a false emphasis, like architectural ornaments in the wrong place. It demands of the reader an imaginative effort where there has been no such effort in the writer, an answering emotion where there is none to be answered. And the reader gets the habit of refusing such effort and such emotion; he ceases even to be aware of metaphors that are used habitually. He may not consciously resent them; but unconsciously his mind is wearied by them as the eye by advertisements often repeated. By their sameness they destroy expectation so that, even if the writer says anything in particular, it seems to be all generalities.

Here is an instance of habitual metaphor, not manufactured for this tract, but taken from an article by a well-known writer. He is speaking of the career of Mr. Lloyd George:

There was nothing like it in the histories of the ancient European monarchies, hide-bound by caste and now lying on the scrap-heaps of Switzerland and Holland. In the more forward nations, the new republics, men have indeed risen from humble beginnings to high station, but not generally by constitutional means and usually only (as now in Russia) by wading to their places through blood. The dizzy height to which Lloyd George has attained, not as a British statesman only but also as a world celebrity, seems to leave the foreign nations breathless. It is a spectacle that has of itself some of the thrill and fascination of romance.

Here are metaphors that might be used, or have been used, so as to surprise the reader; but in this case they are stock-ornaments to a passage that needs no ornament. If the metaphors in the first sentence were alive to us they would be mixed; at least the transition from monarchies hide-bound by caste to monarchies lying on scrap-heaps would be too sudden; but we hardly notice it because we hardly notice the metaphors. And there is an inconsistency in the notion of rising by wading which, again, we do not notice only because we are so used to rising and wading as metaphors that both have lost their power as images. Mr. Lloyd George has waded to such a dizzy height that he seems to leave foreign nations breathless; and we should be breathless at the thought of such an impossibility if the metaphors were not dead.

It is indeed the mark of a dead metaphor that it escapes absurdity only by being dead. The term has been used for metaphors that have lost all metaphorical significance; but these, perhaps, are better called buried metaphors. I prefer to use the word *dead* of metaphors not yet buried but demanding burial. 'Risen from humble beginnings' is perhaps a buried metaphor; 'wading to their places through blood' is a dead one. It has been used so often that it jades instead of horrifying us; it is a corpse that fails to make us think of corpses. But in the next sentence the writer returns to the metaphor of rising and elaborates it so that it is no longer buried, though certainly dead. We are vaguely aware of the sense of this passage, but the metaphors are a hindrance, not a help, to our understanding of it.

Writers fall into habitual metaphor when they fear that their thought will seem too commonplace without ornament; and, because the motive is unconscious, they choose metaphors familiar to themselves and their readers. The article from which I have quoted contains many such metaphors. Mr. Lloyd George is 'like other men only cast in bigger mould'. He is 'clearly no plaster saint'. 'You cannot think of him in relation to the knock-out blow except as the man who gives, not receives, it.' 'He has never lost his head on the dizzy height to which he has so suddenly attained. He is clearly in no danger of the intoxicating impulse of the people who find themselves for the first time on great eminences, to leap over. In a word, he is not spoiled.' Here the writer, as he would put it, gives himself away. All that metaphor means only that Mr. George is not spoiled, and the fact that he is not spoiled would be established better by instances than by metaphors.

Then we are told that some of Mr. George's feats 'seem to partake of the nature of legerdemain'. 'He sways a popular assembly by waves of almost Hebraic emotion.' 'No man has ever had his ear closer to the ground and listened more attentively to the tramp of the oncoming multitudes.' He 'held Great Britain's end up' at the International conference. A 'magnificent tribute was paid to him by Earl Balfour' but it 'did not put him alone on a pinnacle'. And then we read of the whirligig of time, of 'clouds of misunderstanding which point to the coming of a storm'; of how 'foreign nations suddenly became aware that a new star had swum into the world's ken'; of how 'the situation of this country is perilous with so much Bolshevik gunpowder moving about', and how 'it has required a strong heart and a clear head to keep the nation from falling either into the sloughs of despond or the fires of revolution'.

Some of these are metaphors that were excellent in their first use and original context; but they lose their excellence if repeated in any context where they have not been discovered by the emotion of the writer but are used by him to make a commonplace appear passionate. Then they seem an unfortunate legacy from poetry to prose; and it is a fact, I think, that our prose now suffers from the richness of our past poetry. Even the prose writers of the Romantic movement regarded prose as the poor relation of poetry; they did not see that prose has its own reasons for existing, its own state of being and its own beauties. They had the habit of writing about Shakespeare in Shakespeare's own manner, which, in later plays such as *Antony and Cleopatra*, is often a fading of one metaphor into another so fast that the reader's or listener's mind cannot keep pace with it:

O sovereign mistress of true melancholy,
The poisonous damp of night disponge upon me,
That life, a very rebel to my will,
May hang no longer on me: throw my heart
Against the flint and hardness of my fault;
Which, being dried with grief, will break to powder.
And finish all foul thoughts.

The metaphors here, though instinctive rather than habitual, are excessive even for the dying speech of Enobarbus. The style is the worst model for prose, yet it has persisted as a mere habit in the prose of writers who fear to be prosaic and who are prevented by that habit from saying even what they have to say.

The principles of composition, whether verse or prose, are based on the fact that the unit of language is not the word, or even the phrase, but the sentence. From this it follows that every word and every phrase gets its meaning from the sentence in which it occurs; and so that words and phrases should be used freshly on each occasion and, as it were, recharged with meaning by the aptness of their use. Every sentence should, like a piece of music, establish its own relation between the words that compose it; and in the best sentences, whether of prose or verse, the words seem new-born; like notes in music, they seem to be, not mere labels, but facts, because of the manner in which the writer's thought or emotion has related them to each other. But habitual metaphor prevents this process of relation; it is the intrusion of ready-made matter, with its own stale associations, into matter that should be new-made for its own particular purpose of expression. Phrases like—The lap of luxury, Part and parcel, A sea of troubles, Passing through the furnace, Beyond the pale, The battle of life, The death-warrant of, Parrot cries, The sex-war, Tottering thrones, A trail of glory, Bull-dog tenacity, Hats off to, The narrow way, A load of sorrow, A charnel-house, The proud prerogative, Smiling through your tears, A straight fight, A profit and loss account, The fires of martyrdom, The school of life—are all ready-made matter; and, if a writer yields to the temptation of using them, he impedes his own process of expression, saying something which is not exactly what he has to say. He may, of course, attain to a familiar metaphor in his own process of expression; but if he does, if it is exactly what he has to say, then it will not seem stale to the reader. Context may give life to a metaphor that has long seemed dead, as it gives life to the commonest words. If an image forces itself upon a writer because it and it alone will express his meaning, then it is his image, no matter how often it has been used before; and in that case it will arrest the attention of the reader. But the effect of habitual and dead metaphor is to dull attention. When a phrase like 'the lap of luxury' catches the eye, the mind relaxes but is not rested; for we are wearied, without exercise, by commonplace.

Further, the use of dead metaphor weakens a writer's sense of the connexion between mood and manner. All the metaphors which I have quoted are fit for the expression of some kind of emotion rather than for plain statement of fact or for lucid argument; yet they are used commonly in statements of fact and in what passes for argument. Indeed one of their evils is that they make a writer and his readers believe that he is exercising his reason when he is only moving from trite image to image. If eloquence is reason fused with emotion, writing, or speaking, full of dead metaphors is unreason fused with sham emotion. I add in illustration a further list of dead metaphors lately noticed: 'Branches of the same deadly Upas Tree. Turning a deaf ear to. The flower of our manhood. Taking off the gloves. Written in letters of fire. Stemming the tide. Big with possibilities. The end is in sight. A place in the sun. A spark of manhood. To dry up the founts of pity. Hunger stalking through the land. A death grip. Round pegs (or men) in square holes. The lamp of sacrifice. The silver lining. Troubling the waters, and poisoning the wells. The promised land. Flowing with milk and honey. Winning all along the line. Casting in her lot with. The fruits of victory. Backs to the wall. Bubbling over with confidence. Bled white. The writing on the wall. The sickle of death. A ring fence round. The crucible of. Answering the call. Grinding the faces of the poor. The scroll of fame.'—A. CLUTTON-BROCK.

IRRELEVANT ALLUSION

We all know the people—for they are the majority, and probably include our particular selves—who cannot carry on the ordinary business of everyday talk without the use of phrases containing a part that is appropriate, and another that is pointless or worse; the two parts have associated themselves together in their minds as making up what somebody has said, and what others as well as they will find familiar, and they have the sort of pleasure in producing the combination that a child has in airing a newly acquired word. There is, indeed, a certain charm in the grown man's boyish ebullience, not to be restrained by thoughts of relevance from letting the exuberant phrase jet forth. And for that charm we put up with it when a speaker draws our attention to the methodical by telling us there is a method in the madness, though method and not madness is all there is to see, when another's every winter is the winter of his discontent, when a third cannot complain of the light without calling it religious as well as dim, when for a fourth nothing can be rotten outside the State of Denmark, or when a fifth, asked whether he does not owe you 1s. 6d. for that cab fare, owns the soft impeachment.

A slightly fuller examination of a single example may be useful. The phrase to *leave severely alone* has two reasonable uses—one in the original sense of to leave alone as a method of severe treatment, i.e. to send to Coventry or show contempt for, and the other in contexts where *severely* is to be interpreted by contraries—to leave alone by way not of punishing the object, but of avoiding consequences for the subject. The straightforward meaning, and the ironical, are both good; anything between them, in which the real meaning is merely to leave alone, and *severely* is no more than an echo, is pointless and vapid and in print intolerable. Examples follow: (1, straightforward) *You must show him, by leaving him severely alone, by putting him into a moral Coventry, your detestation of the crime*; (2, ironical) *Fish of prey do not appear to relish the sharp spines of the stickleback, and usually seem to leave them severely alone*; (3, pointless) *Austria forbids children to smoke in public places; and in German schools and military colleges there are laws upon the subject; France, Spain, Greece, and Portugal leave the matter severely alone.* It is obvious at once how horrible the faded jocularity of No. 3 is in print; and, though things like it come crowding upon one another in most conversation, they are not very easy to find in newspapers and books of any merit; a small gleaning of them follows:

The moral, as Alice would say, *appeared to be that, despite its difference in degree, an obvious essential in the right kind of education had been equally lacking to both these girls* (as Alice, or indeed as you or I, might say).

Resignation became a virtue of necessity *for Sweden* (If you do what you must with a good grace, you make a virtue of necessity; without *make*, a virtue of necessity loses its meaning).

I strongly advise the single working-man who would become a successful backyard poultry-keeper to ignore the advice of Punch, *and to secure a useful helpmate.*

The beloved lustige Wien [merry Vienna] *of his youth had* suffered a sea-change. *The green glacis ... was blocked by ranges of grand new buildings* (Ariel must chuckle at the odd places in which his sea-change turns up).

Many of the celebrities who in that most frivolous of watering-places do congregate.

When about to quote Sir Oliver Lodge's tribute to the late leader, Mr. Law drew, not a dial, *but what was obviously a penny memorandum book* from his pocket (You want to mention that Mr. Bonar Law took a notebook out of his pocket. But pockets are humdrum things. How give a literary touch? Call it a poke? No, we can better that; who was it drew what from his poke? Why, Touchstone, a dial, to be sure! and there you are).—H.W.F.

CORRESPONDENCE

We have a constant flow of correspondence, and we are afraid the writers must think us unpractical, incompetent, or neglectful, because we give their inquiries no place in our tracts; they may naturally think that it is our business to pass judgement on any linguistic question that troubles them; but most of these queries would be satisfactorily answered by reference to the O. E. D., which we do not undertake to reprint; in other cases, where we are urged to protest against the common abuse of some word or phrase, we do not think (as we have before explained) that it is worth while to treat any such detail without full illustration, and this our correspondents do not supply. We propose now to demonstrate the situation by dealing with a small selection of these abused words, which may serve as examples.

* * * * *

IMPLICIT

The human mind likes a good clear black-and-white contrast; when two words so definitely promise one of these contrasts as *explicit* and *implicit*, and then dash our hopes by figuring in phrases where contrast ceases to be visible—say in 'explicit support' and 'implicit obedience', with *absolute* or *complete* or *full* as a substitute that might replace either or both—, we ask with some indignation whether after all black is white, and perhaps decide that *implicit* is a shifty word with which we will have no further dealings. It is noteworthy in more than one respect.

First, it means for the most part the same as *implied*, and, as it is certainly not so instantly intelligible to the average man, it might have been expected to be so good as to die. That it has nevertheless survived by the side of *implied* is perhaps due to two causes: one is that *explicit* and *implicit* make a neater antithesis than even *expressed* and *implied* (we should write *all the conditions, whether explicit or implicit;* but *all the implied conditions; implied* being much commoner than *implicit* when the antithesis is not given in full); and the other is that the adverb, whether of *implicit* or of *implied*, is more often wanted than the adjective, and that *impliedly* is felt to be a bad form; *implicitly*, preferred to *impliedly*, helps to keep *implicit* alive.

Secondly, there is the historical accident by which *implicit*, with *faith, obedience, confidence*, and such words, has come to mean absolute or full, whereas it originally meant undeveloped or potential or in the germ. The starting-point of this usage is the ecclesiastical phrase *implicit faith*, i.e. a person's acceptance of any article of belief not on its own merits, but as a part of, as 'wrapped up in', his general acceptance of the Church's authority; the steps from this sense to unquestioning, and thence to complete or absolute or exact, are easy; but not every one who says that implicit obedience is the first duty of the soldier realizes that the obedience he is describing is not properly an exact one, but one that is involved in acceptance of the soldier's status.—[H.W.F.]

It seems to us (by virtue of this 'historical accident') that in such a phrase as the *implied* or *implicit conditions* of a contract, there is a recognized difference of meaning in the two words. *Implied* conditions, though unexpressed, need not be hidden, they are rather such as any one who agreed to the main stipulation would recognize as involved; and the word *implied* might even carry the plea that they were unspecified because openly apparent. On the other hand *implicit* conditions are rather such as are unsuspected and in a manner hidden.—[ED.]

PRACTICALLY

A correspondent complains that the adverb 'almost' is being supplanted by 'practically'. 'The true meaning of "practically" (he writes) is "in practice" as opposed to "in theory" or "in thought"; for instance, *Questions which are theoretically interesting to thoughtful people and practically to every one*, or again, *He loves himself contemplatively by knowing as he is known and practically by loving as he is loved.*' And he finds fault with the *O.E.D.*, whence he takes his quotations, for not condemning such phrases as these, *The application was supported by practically all the creditors*, and, *He has been very ill but is now practically well again.*

The word is no doubt abused and intrudes everywhere. *The Times* writes of a recent gale, *Considerable damage was done by the gale in practically every parish in Jersey*, and again of a bridge on the Seine that *The structure has practically been swept away*; but it seems that in the sense of 'for practical purposes' it can be defended as a useful word. For instance, a friend, leaving your house at night to walk home, says, *It is full moon, isn't it?* and you reply *Practically*, meaning that it is full enough for his purpose. You might say *nearabouts* or *thereabouts* or *sufficiently*, but you cannot say *almost* or *nearly* without implying that you know the full moon to be nearly due and not past. In such cases it might be argued that 'practically' is truly opposed to 'theoretically', but 'actually' is rather its opposite. 'Practically' implies an undefined margin of error which does not affect the situation.

LITERALLY

A correspondent quotes: *For the last three years I literally coined money*, and, *My hair literally stood on end*. The common misuse of this word is so absurd that it would not be worth while to protest against it, if its daily appearance in every newspaper did not show that it was tolerated by educated people. Mr. Fowler writes:

'We have come to such a pass with this emphasizer that where the truth would require us to acknowledge our exaggeration with, "not literally, of course, but in a manner of speaking", we do not hesitate to insert the very word that we ought to be at pains to repudiate; such false coin makes honest traffic in words impossible. *If the Home Rule Bill is passed, the 300,000 Unionists of the South and West of Ireland will be* literally thrown to the wolves. *The strong "tête-de-pont" fortifications were rushed by our troops, and a battalion crossed the bridge* literally on the enemy's shoulders. In both, *practically* or *virtually*, opposites of *literally*, would have stood.'

INFINITELY

This word, like *infiniment* in French, is commonly used for 'extremely', and it is pedantic to object to it by insisting always on its full logical meaning; but it should be avoided where measurable quantities are spoken of; for instance, one may say *to indoctrinate the mob with philosophical notions does infinite harm,* but to say that *England is infinitely more populous than Australia* is absurd. That one can rightly call atoms infinitely small means that they are to our senses immeasurable, and the word, as it here carries wonder, may, like other conversational expletives, have an emotional force, and can therefore be sometimes well used even where its exaggeration is apparent. As when a man heightens some assertion with a 'damnable,' he intends by the colour of his speech to warn you that his conviction is profound, and that he is in no mood to listen to reason, so the exaggeration of 'infinite' may have special value by giving emotional colour to a sentence.

On the above principles there will be doubtful cases. For instance, was Mr. Lloyd George justified the other day in saying, *If you cut down expenditure to the lowest possible limit, the war debt would still be so enormous that ... the expenditure for this country is bound to be infinitely greater than before the war?*—*The Times,* Oct. 23.

THE AMERICAN INVITATION

The English reply to the American Invitation was despatched last October. The text of it is as follows:

'To Professor Fred Newton Scott.

DEAR SIR,

We thank you heartily for the letter addressed to us by Professors James Wilson Bright, Albert Stanburrough Cook, Charles Hall Grandgent, Robert Underwood Johnson, John Livingston Lowes, John Matthews Manly, Charles Grosvenor Osgood, and yourself.

We regret that so long a time should have passed before our joint reply could be despatched: but our intentions have in the meanwhile been privately made known to you. We now write to give you formal assurance of the interest and sympathy with which your proposal has been received, and to thank you for your generous suggestion that we in the mother country of our language should take the lead in furthering the project.

Since then we, both Americans and British, are in complete agreement as to our aims, we have only to decide on the best means and devise the best machinery that we can to attain them.

We feel that this practical question needs very careful consideration and consultation: and we have therefore appointed a small committee of five persons on our side to confer and draw up a table of suggestions which can be submitted to you. We would invite you on your side to take a similar step: we could then compare our respective proposals and agree upon a basis on which to work. There are two dangers which we feel it especially desirable to avoid: one is the establishment of an authoritative academy, tending inevitably to divorce the literary from the spoken language; the other is the creation of a body so large as to be unmanageable. We have also to cope with the difficulty of co-ordinating the activities of members representing many branches in widely scattered territories. Our committee for consultation on these matters consists of Henry Bradley, Robert Bridges, A.T.Q. Couch, Henry Newbolt, and J. Dover Wilson: and we shall be glad if you can tell us that you approve of our preliminary step and will be willing to consider our suggestions when they are ready.

> (Signed) BALFOUR.
> ROBERT BRIDGES.
> HENRY NEWBOLT.'

A first meeting of the consulting committee mentioned in the above reply was held in Corpus Christi College, Oxford, on Nov. 1st ult.

Present: Henry Bradley, Robert Bridges, Sir Henry Newbolt, and J. Dover Wilson.

Discussion was confined to practical questions of organization, and Sir Henry Newbolt undertook to draft a letter in which the sense of